Ten F
for S{

Candlestick Press

Published by:

Candlestick Press,

Diversity House, 72 Nottingham Road, Arnold, Nottingham NG5 6LF

www.candlestickpress.co.uk

Design and typesetting by Craig Twigg

Printed by Ratcliff & Roper Print Group, Nottinghamshire, UK

Selection © Di Slaney and Katharine Towers

Introduction © Katharine Towers

Cover illustration © Alexandra Buckle, 2020
www.alexandrabuckle.co.uk

Candlestick Press monogram © Barbara Shaw, 2008
© Candlestick Press, 2020

ISBN 978 1 907598 96 8

Acknowledgements

The poems in this pamphlet are reprinted from the following books, all by permission of the publishers listed unless stated otherwise. Every effort has been made to trace the copyright holders of the poems published in this book. The editor and publisher apologise if any material has been included without permission or without the appropriate acknowledgement, and would be glad to be told of anyone who has not been consulted.

Thanks are due to all the copyright holders cited below for their kind permission:

Nichola Deane, *Cuckoo* (V. Press, 2019, ISBN: 978-1-9165052-4-7) by kind permission of the author and publisher. Valerie Gillies, *The Cream of the Well* (Luath Press, 2004). Jessica Mookherjee, poem first published in this pamphlet. Alicia Ostriker, *The Old Woman, the Tulip, and the Dog* (University of Pittsburgh Press, 2014) by kind permission of the author and publisher.

All permissions cleared courtesy of Swift Permissions
swiftpermissions@gmail.com

Where poets are no longer living their dates are given.

Contents

		Page
Introduction		5
Loveliest of trees, the cherry now	*AE Housman*	7
Dear March – Come in –	*Emily Dickinson*	8
Frog Spring	*Valerie Gillies*	9
Spring	*Edna St. Vincent Millay*	10
April	*Alicia Ostriker*	11
Hero Worship	*Jessica Mookherjee*	12
The Spring	*Thomas Carew*	13
Home Pictures in May	*John Clare*	14
Cuckoo	*Nichola Deane*	15
Spring	*Gerard Manley Hopkins*	16

Introduction

Spring – season of some of poetry's most memorable moments. There's something about the exuberance and hopefulness of new growth and returning warmth that seems to make poets want to pick up their pens.

This selection includes one poem that we just couldn't do without. Housman's rhapsody to cherry blossom (tinged with the melancholy of passing time) is a piece that slides effortlessly into the memory. The other choices are less well-known and we hope there will be some delightful surprises for the reader. From Nichola Deane's "souped up" modern cuckoo casting its spell over the greenwood to Edna St. Vincent Millay's irreverent take on April, these are poems of varied and sometimes unexpected moods.

Jessica Mookherjee's poem also finds us in April. Spring is, of course, the season of love and here we meet a young girl smitten by a glamorous man who meets her at the school gate in his sports car. The poem ends with a glancingly ironic reference to TS Eliot's "cruellest" month. Equally modern in tone is Alicia Ostriker's poem, in which spring is encountered in an urban setting where new buds compete for attention with traffic and the overflowing waste bins in a city park.

The selection wouldn't be complete without a poem by perhaps the greatest ever poet of the natural world, John Clare. Here you'll find one of his paeans to the month of May: a lovely sonnet that takes the reader by the hand to look at daffodils, goslings and a robin waiting for the gardener to turn up a worm.

Whether or not you agree with Gerard Manley Hopkins whose concluding poem here declares that "Nothing is so beautiful as spring –" we hope you will enjoy this rich and varied celebration of what is perhaps the most miraculous and irresistible season of the year.

Katharine Towers

Loveliest of trees, the cherry now

Loveliest of trees, the cherry now
Is hung with bloom along the bough,
And stands about the woodland ride
Wearing white for Eastertide.

Now, of my threescore years and ten,
Twenty will not come again,
And take from seventy springs a score,
It only leaves me fifty more.

And since to look at things in bloom
Fifty springs are little room,
About the woodlands I will go
To see the cherry hung with snow.

AE Housman (1859 – 1936)

Dear March – Come in –

Dear March – Come in –
How glad I am –
I hoped for you before –
Put down your Hat –
You must have walked –
How out of Breath you are –
Dear March, how are you, and the Rest –
Did you leave Nature well –
Oh March, Come right upstairs with me –
I have so much to tell –

I got your Letter, and the Birds –
The Maples never knew that you were coming –
I declare – how Red their Faces grew –
But March, forgive me –
And all those Hills you left for me to Hue –
There was no Purple suitable –
You took it all with you –

Who knocks? That April –
Lock the Door –
I will not be pursued –
He stayed away a Year to call
When I am occupied –
But trifles look so trivial
As soon as you have come

That blame is just as dear as Praise
And Praise as mere as Blame –

Emily Dickinson (1830 – 1886)

Frog Spring

Surprised by my tasting the spring, a golden frog
leaps to the bank. He flies to froggy places,
his ankle-joints stretch the moment.

A puddock from his pop-eyes to his paddle-toes,
he darts out of the vital pool. Immortal frog,
to see him so healthy is a sure sign

the spring will do the same for me.
He hops past my shoulder into the paddy-pipes,
the reed-bed pockets frog. He vanishes through,
each spear of rush keeps its own drop of dew.

Valerie Gillies

Spring

To what purpose, April, do you return again?
Beauty is not enough.
You can no longer quiet me with the redness
Of little leaves opening stickily.
I know what I know.
The sun is hot on my neck as I observe
The spikes of the crocus.
The smell of the earth is good.
It is apparent that there is no death.
But what does that signify?
Not only under ground are the brains of men
Eaten by maggots.
Life in itself
Is nothing,
An empty cup, a flight of uncarpeted stairs.
It is not enough that yearly, down this hill,
April
Comes like an idiot, babbling and strewing flowers.

Edna St. Vincent Millay (1892 – 1950)

April

The optimists among us
taking heart because it is spring
skip along
attending their meetings
signing their email petitions
marching with their satiric signs
singing their give peace a chance songs
posting their rainbow twitters and blogs
believing in a better world
for no good reason
I envy them
said the old woman

The seasons go round they
go round and around
said the tulip
swaying among her friends
in their brown bed in the sun
in the April breeze
under a maple canopy
that was also dancing
only with greater motions
casting greater shadows
and the grass
hardly stirring

What a concerto
of good stinks said the dog
trotting along Riverside Drive
in the early spring afternoon
sniffing this way and that
how gratifying the violins of the river
the tubas of the traffic
the trombones
of the leafing elms with the legato
of my rivals' piss at their feet
and the leftover meat and grease
singing along in all the wastebaskets

Alicia Ostriker

Hero Worship

Achilles picked me up from school in his red sports car.
Spring term, buds were out, my shirt buttons
undone and skirt hitched up. *Get in* he said, sounding American,
I swooned as the girls turned. He looked through our smiles,
and told me in a whisper that I looked like Taylor Swift.

I walked down hallways looking for him, wrote his name
on my pencil case, swore blind, made excuses, like some poor fool,
spent my days cutting him out of magazines. He was drunk
with Pat in the dark dive bars, opposite the station, where I found him
and he told me in a whisper I was wasting my time.

So I got all love bitten on a sugar-coated neck as he sent
me love songs on the internet and hired a man to write in the sky
with a plane, my name, asking to take me back. I smiled to myself
as he bled from his heals and showed things to Pat no girl
should reveal. It was spring and my step had a mean, mean streak.

The girls, all creamed up with strawberry lip-gloss, crossed their legs
in bobby-socks, watched me out of the sides of their eyes.
Achilles picked me up on his motor bike, outside the school gates, down
narrow lanes, on lines of speed and acid tabs. It was April
and he told me I was a cruel, cruel girl to tease him like that.

Jessica Mookherjee

The Spring

Now that the winter's gone, the earth hath lost
Her snow-white robes, and now no more the frost
Candies the grass, or casts an icy cream
Upon the silver lake or crystal stream;
But the warm sun thaws the benumbéd earth,
And makes it tender, gives a sacred birth
To the dead swallow, wakes in hollow tree
The drowsy cuckoo and the humble bee.
Now do a choir of chirping minstrels bring
In triumph to the world the youthful spring.
The valleys, hills, and woods in rich array
Welcome the coming of the long'd-for May.
Now all things smile: only my love doth lour,
Nor hath the scalding noonday sun the power
To melt that marble ice which still doth hold
Her heart congeal'd, and makes her pity cold.
The ox, which lately did for shelter fly
Into the stall, doth now securely lie
In open fields; and love no more is made
By the fireside, but in the cooler shade:
Amyntas now doth with his Chloris sleep
Under a sycamore, and all things keep
Time with the season. Only she doth carry
June in her eyes, in her heart January.

Thomas Carew (1595 – 1640)

Home Pictures in May

The sunshine bathes in clouds of many hues
And mornings feet are gemmed with early dews
Warm Daffodils about the garden beds
Peep thro their pale slim leaves their golden heads
Sweet earthly suns of spring – the Gosling broods
In coats of sunny green about the road
Waddle in extacy – and in rich moods
The old hen leads her flickering chicks abroad
Oft scuttling neath her wings to see the kite
Hang wavering oer them in the springs blue light
The sparrows round their new nests chirp with glee
And sweet the Robin springs young luxury shares
Tuteling its song in feathery Goosberry tree
While watching worms the Gardeners spade unbears

John Clare (1793 – 1864)

Cuckoo

When the buds
on the birch
disappear

I appear
      so spooked,
het-up,

heaven-fretted,
bejesused,
souped up

with all the may-
bees in May,
the new

plight of the new
(Cuckoo,
Cuccu)

to *haunt* us
back,
to the sleeping

greenwood
(like that, how so?)
with a – wake for a voice,

my loopy echo,
a bit of
locus pocus

Nichola Deane

Spring

Nothing is so beautiful as spring –
    When weeds, in wheels, shoot long and lovely and lush;
    Thrush's eggs look little low heavens, and thrush
Through the echoing timber does so rinse and wring
The ear, it strikes like lightnings to hear him sing;
    The glassy peartree leaves and blooms, they brush
    The descending blue; that blue is all in a rush
With richness; the racing lambs too have fair their fling.

What is all this juice and all this joy?
    A strain of the earth's sweet being in the beginning
In Eden garden. – Have, get, before it cloy,
    Before it cloud, Christ, lord, and sour with sinning,
Innocent mind and Mayday in girl and boy,
    Most, O maid's child, thy choice and worthy the winning.

Gerard Manley Hopkins (1844 – 1889)